"I find the Booster Breaks very relaxing. My productivity seems to increase following the break and that's very important to me. Health benefits would be great, but the mental health benefits and relaxation are what I really appreciate."

Alicia Gladney ~ Booster Break participant

"Beginning a health promotion program is challenging when you're faced with limited resources and precious little time each day. Yet we did, and we are proud to be the first to complete a year-long Booster Break program here at Carol Davis Reporting. Try starting a Booster Break program in your workplace. You'll find results like improved individual morale, and enhanced team spirit are surprising value-added benefits to this positive, healthy program. This is the book that will help your organization develop its own Booster Break program."

Alice Farrack, Vice President Operations
Carol Davis Reporting, Records & Video, Inc.

"The Booster Break experience meant positive results for me. Sure, fifteen minutes of daily exercise does a body well, but what I didn't expect was how the Booster Break fostered better communication and team cohesion among my colleagues and me. Participating in the Booster Break also reinforced company leadership positively among all participants. Finally, the Booster Break prompted me to re-evaluate exercise and adopt it as a valued and necessary component of my everyday life."

Karl Grube ~ Booster Break participant

"It's exciting to have the book, Booster Breaks: Improving Employee Health One Break at a Time. Corporate America is in desperate need of this book! With health care costs spiraling upward and productivity, creativity, and morale plummeting (thanks to sedentary lifestyles), it's a gift to have a powerful solution through such a simple, natural means. As a corporate wellness consultant and executive coach, I wholeheartedly recommend this book as a requirement for any corporation that desires increased productivity and profitability, coupled with reduced health care costs. Pick up a copy of the book and start implementing the program today!"

Salvatore Fichera, MEd
Corporate Wellness Consultant & Coach
Author of Stop Aging, Start Training

"As a business consultant and fitness trainer, I firmly believe that, Booster Breaks: Improving Employee Health One Break at a Time, is a resource that will greatly benefit my clients and their employees. Booster Breaks are a great way to include health promotion at the work site. This manual is the definitive guide for implementing an effective Booster Break program."

Ellen Taer, MPH
Fitness Consultant (25 years experience)

"When I signed up for the Booster Break Study, I had no idea of the impact that it would have on me. I initially thought it would be a nuisance, but it probably would get me out of the office for a change. So when the program began, I was not expecting much and thought to myself, 'Will this keep my interest for an extended period of time?' Well, to my surprise this Booster Break Study immediately became a catalyst that encouraged me to get on a regular exercise program and make an effort to aid myself by becoming more physically active, in spite of being a middle-aged, immensely overweight, unhealthy man. As time passed, I found myself not only enthusiastically participating, but also disappointed when I could not participate.

As a result of this nudge given by the Booster Break, I now have dropped 70 pounds and feel as though I am becoming a new person with a new life viewpoint. I say without hesitation that as the pounds have dropped, my energy has increased and I credit the Booster Break with igniting a fire in me."

Nathaniel Jones ~ Booster Break Participant

Booster Breaks:

Improving Employee Health
One Break at a Time

Wendell C. Taylor, PhD, MPH
Karen L. Pepkin, MA

Booster Breaks:
Improving Employee Health One Break at a Time

Published by:
Karrick Press
P.O. Box 772027
Houston, Texas 77215

For more information on Booster Breaks, and resources for your Booster Breaks program, visit us on the Internet at http://www.BoosterBreaksBook.com.

Printed in the United States of America
ISBN: 978-0-578-05975-4

Our book is dedicated to family and loved ones
who have passed away: Charles Lee Taylor,
Myer (Mike) Pepkin, Esther Scherick Pepkin,
and Aviva Stone.
Also, our book is dedicated to
Birdell Thurston Taylor
who continues to inspire.

Acknowledgements

We acknowledge Alice Farrack and her staff at Carol Davis Court Reporting, Houston, Texas, the first official Booster Break organization. Also, we acknowledge Sandra Ahlhorn, Speedy Printing, Houston, Texas, for her review, Suzy Scannell for her eagle eye proof reading, Dr. Ken Goodrick for his review, Cathy Stucker for her invaluable assistance in publishing the book and Julie Howell, Studiojules.com, for her design of the book. Finally, we are grateful to the individuals who provided testimonials and all Booster Break participants.

Contents

Part I

"Only those who risk going too far
can possibly find out
how far they can go."
T.S. Elliot

1
Introduction

Life today is complicated. It seems we are asked to do more with less time, less money, and less support. Although meditation has been shown to reduce stress and have a positive impact on health, most of us do not meditate on a regular basis. Similarly, it is common knowledge that physical activity is beneficial, yet studies show that less than 15% of people engage in 30 minutes of physical activity five or more days per week as recommended by the Surgeon General of the United States and national health organizations (US Department of Health and Human Services; Healthy People, 2010).

Health clubs look forward to January when people make their New Year's resolutions, yet six months later only a small percent of those who joined still attend regularly. One reason may be that making a change is an admirable goal but difficult to sustain. Stores abound with books, CDs, and DVDs on these topics; however, the perception is that meditation and physical activity require time that cannot be taken from other daily responsibilities.

For a majority of people, a large part of their day is spent at the workplace, so what happens at the work place can have tremendous implications for health. Many people cite the job as a stressor. Others are sedentary the majority of the day. Both stress and sedentary behavior compromise health (Taylor, 2005). Given the time spent at work, why not create an easy to implement alternative to promote health at the work place? Some companies offer programs before or after work hours, on-site facilities to make exercise more accessible, or provide health-related seminars during lunch. Even though these efforts are important and some employees take advantage of them, others do not for a variety of reasons. A solution is needed that is more universal and can serve as a basis for a routine practice that is easy to implement and convenient for all employees. Standard break times are an underutilized opportunity to promote health and enhance well-being. The Booster Break is a practical solution to this dilemma.

WHAT IS A BOOSTER BREAK?

Booster Breaks are a new way of thinking about work breaks. The formal definition is an "organized, routine, work break intended to improve physical and psychological health, enhance organizational morale, and sustain or increase work productivity" (Taylor, 2005).

This formal definition conveys only a part of the meaning of this innovative concept and paradigm shift.

Booster Breaks provide an opportunity for employees to engage in health-promoting behaviors during the work day that can be performed in work clothes. Typically break time means consuming coffee, tea, or other drinks, surfing the net, eating unhealthy snacks, or smoking cigarettes. Our vision for the future is that Booster Breaks will be as accepted as the current health-compromising practices. Our hope is that this book will serve as a catalyst for a change in norms related to break times.

For a majority of people, a large part of their day is spent at the workplace, so what happens at the work place can have tremendous implications for health.

2
How Did All This Get Started?

Have you ever taken a tour of a factory? Three years ago, we took a tour of a famous ice cream factory in Texas. As we observed workers performing their duties on the conveyer belt, we noticed that break-times were systematic and organized. One group left the conveyer belt as another group took its place. The next week as we drove by one of the largest medical centers in the world, we saw staff smoking outside a cancer hospital. The following week over 50 threaded e-mails were received seeking recommendations for various types of coffee (including costs and potential vendors) to determine which selection would be provided for coffee breaks. These observations made us realize that break times were embedded in our culture with smoking, coffee, and other health compromising practices accepted as the norm.

In the United States, many labor contracts require two 15-minute breaks (one in the morning and one in the afternoon). Initially, these breaks were used for smoking, consuming coffee, and snacking. Over time, other practices have become common such as surfing the internet and making personal phone calls.

In contrast, Asian societies routinely practice physical movements such as Tai Chi in the morning or afternoon and many Latin American and European cultures still observe siesta breaks during lunch time.

Since break times are a standard part of many employees' work day, what happens during break times can have implications for work productivity and employee health. In recent times, two dominant public health trends have emerged, the obesity epidemic and stress at the workplace. These trends are a great concern to the public in general, because it affects everyday lives and for public health scientists, these trends are particularly disturbing.

Given the confluence of these observations, coupled with public health trends, it became clear that break times could be used to promote health for the general public. Therefore, we wrote a scientific paper that was published in the American Journal of Preventive Medicine (a leading journal in medicine and public health). In this paper, we proposed the Booster Break and underscored the fact that work breaks are an underutilized opportunity for health promotion. The concept of the Booster Break has resonated with scientists, the popular press, business periodicals and also has been posted on websites (see appendix). The reactions to and interest in the Booster Break concept inspired us to write this book so that companies of any size can implement the Booster Break program.

Traditional Break Time Activities
- Consuming Coffee
- Smoking Cigarettes
- Consuming Unhealthy Snacks
- Surfing the Internet

Booster Break Activities
- Physical Activity
(e.g., Stretching, Tai Chi, Yoga, etc.)
- Meditation
- Relaxation Techniques
- Rhythmic Breathing
- Consuming Healthy Foods

3
What Will it Take for
My Organization to Get Started?

What you don't need to get started:
- Elaborate equipment
- Large commitment of time
- Purchase of additional resources
- Out-of-pocket expenses
- Current healthy lifestyle practices
- Special athletic clothing

What you do need to get started:
- Wellness culture assessment
- Management support
- Employee buy-in
- Appropriate Booster Break selection

WELLNESS CULTURE ASSESSMENT

Some companies include a statement about health and wellness in their mission statement, because they see

22

it as a value for their company. Other companies may not explicitly mention it, but their policies exemplify a concern for the whole person, and still others are silent or have not considered this aspect of workplace life. Irrespective of where the organization is on this continuum, there are scales to formally assess the wellness culture of the organization. A scale can be obtained at the following website. http://BoosterBreaksBook.com/assessment

In addition to the formal scale, workplace culture can be assessed informally by obtaining information related to the following:

Does your organization have a Wellness Department?

A Wellness Director and/or Wellness Department help to insure that practices and policies of the organization are consistent with promoting health. They coordinate workshops, provide support for lifestyle change, and offer personal counseling services. Also, they monitor and evaluate organizational programs related to wellness.

Does your organization have a mission statement that values wellness?

Whether your organization does or does not have a wellness department, it may still have wellness as an organizational value as reflected in the mission statement.

Does your organization provide a workout facility?
Some organizations have a workout facility on site or may offer discounts to local health clubs or gyms to encourage employees to be physically active.

Does your organization routinely hold sessions or events on health-related topics?
In some organizations, there are expert presentations to help employees improve their health. These presentations cover the most recent research, practical tips, motivation to change lifestyle, and resources to provide support.

The primary purpose of assessing the health and wellness culture is to determine the organization's willingness to embrace the Booster Break concept. Based on these assessments, if wellness is not a priority for your organization, then more preliminary work may be appropriate to increase the organization's receptivity to Booster Breaks.

MANAGEMENT SUPPORT
Systemic change requires management support at all levels to be successful. Understanding what it takes to win

management support at your company is the first step. Sometimes it is data; sometimes it is persuasion based on the company's goals and objectives; sometimes it is being consistent with the company's vision, such as being an innovator. Convincing management may initially take some time, however the end results are worth the effort. Below are some of the approaches that can be considered.

Meet individually with management representatives

Some organizations have an open door policy where employees can easily express concerns and make suggestions directly to management. If this situation reflects your organizational culture, employees can formally or informally advise management about the potential benefits of Booster Breaks. In approaching management, supportive data can help strengthen your case, so be sure to carefully review this book before using this approach.

Make presentations to leadership teams

Many organizations have management teams that meet on a regular basis to discuss organizational matters and make decisions. One strategy is to request permission to make a brief presentation. In this way, the decision makers can learn about the potential benefits of the Booster Break and decide as a team to support it. Additionally, this approach could generate interest throughout the entire organization.

Write persuasively to management to engender their support

The structure of some organizations does not allow employees direct access to decision makers. Also, some employees may not feel comfortable making persuasive presentations. In this case, putting a recommendation in the suggestion box or writing a letter/email explaining all aspects of the Booster Break and its potential benefits to employers and employees may be an effective strategy.

Collect data to show employee interest in the Booster Break

Employee interest can be an essential aspect of persuading management to adopt a Booster Break program. Presenting a petition, results from surveys, or some other means of collecting data can provide documentation to show employee interest.

Typically, management is concerned with benefits and costs of any endeavor. In order to persuade management to adopt Booster Breaks, benefits and costs must be addressed. Below is information that relates to both of these areas:

Productivity and time away from work

Managers may be concerned about employees taking too many breaks or spending too much time at breaks, and the negative impact on productivity. One scientific study *(Galinsky, et al., 2007)* directly addressed whether the number of and time spent during break time decreased productivity. This study was completed with data entry operators who worked for the Internal Revenue Service in Cincinnati, Ohio. One group of operators had the standard two 15-minute breaks, one in the morning and one in the afternoon. A second group had the standard two 15-minute breaks plus four additional breaks of five minutes each *(20 additional break minutes)*. During the five-minute breaks, the data entry operators were expected to do stretching exercises. At the end of the day, the group with the additional 20 minutes of breaks, had significantly faster keystroke speed and produced as many documents as the other group, who worked 20 minutes longer. The authors concluded that the additional breaks reduced fatigue and strain.

Employee stress

For many employees the workplace creates unhealthy stress *(Steenland et al., 2000)*. Several studies have shown that relaxation and meditation techniques *(a Booster Break option) (Davidson et al., 2003)* can reduce counterproductive stress.

Organizational morale

In Norway, instituting discussion groups based on the "Chicken Soup" book series was studied to assess stress reduction. Stress was reduced and the discussions did improve employees' opinion of the company and in so doing, improved organizational morale because the workers perceived the company as caring about them beyond their work output (Horan, 2002).

Promoting health

It has been shown that 15 minutes of physical activity has health benefits including reducing the risk of diabetes and hypertension, and improving heart health (Surgeon General's Report on Physical Activity and Health and Healthy People 2010).

Creating a culture consistent with company values

If part of an organization's mission is to develop a

wellness culture, then a Booster Break program is consistent with this mission.

STRATEGIES TO PERSUADE MANAGEMENT

If there is a Wellness Department *(which is more typical of large organizations)*, then the director and staff of this department should take the lead in persuading senior management of the value and advantages of Booster Breaks. By knowing the culture of the company and having credibility, the Wellness Department staff can develop effective strategies to enlist the support of senior management.

If your organization does not have a Wellness Department, another approach is a grassroots movement stemming from employee interest. An employee survey to assess interest in the Booster Break is another viable strategy. If there is strong employee interest, these data can be compelling in obtaining support from senior management.

In addition to a grassroots movement, scientific data can be persuasive. Throughout this book, we have cited various research studies that support the potential of Booster Breaks.

Productivity

There are limited empirical data about work breaks

and physical activity. Taylor *(2005)* reviewed the literature related to these two areas. In general, the literature indicates that more short term work breaks lead to greater productivity. Based on empirical data, the bottom line is that work breaks have not resulted in decreased productivity and may actually lead to increased productivity *(Galinsky et al., 2005)*.

Boosting Morale

Employees in some companies believe that their management views their employees as production units, and not as whole people. In fact a study from Norway previously cited showed that a program designed to reduce employee stress did have a positive effect on increasing organizational morale because of the perception that the company cared about the employees as individuals (Horan, 2002). In addition to organizational morale, Booster Breaks can increase camaraderie among employees by providing common non-work-related activities that can help employees bond.

Stress Reduction

The activities proposed for Booster Breaks are physical activity, meditation, relaxation, and breath training. Any of these activities practiced on a regular basis have been shown to decrease stress, improve the immune system, and promote healthy living *(Taylor 2005; Brown & Gerbarg, 2005)*. Stress is a common complaint at the worksite; therefore the source of stress *(workplace demands)* should also provide opportunities to relieve stress.

EMPLOYEE BUY-IN

To ensure the success of the Booster Break program, employees should be eager, ready, or at least receptive to participating. In some cases, employees may request organized health-promoting work breaks after hearing about successful Booster Break programs. In other cases, employees initially may be less enthusiastic. In this situation, information about the benefits of health-promoting work breaks and awareness of how these breaks can fit into the work day are essential to prepare participants for this new experience.

Making Work Fun

Today everyone knows that healthy practices should be a part of your daily routine, but beginning to be physically active, meditate, or even make healthy food choices can seem overwhelming. The Booster Break allows employees to begin the process by making it not only easy to implement, but enjoyable as well.

Making small changes in health practices allows the employee to try out new behaviors without incurring the expense of joining a health club or paying for a class. It's a low-risk venture. If the employee enjoys the activity, the hope is that the Booster Break can serve as a catalyst to create changes outside the workplace. Having social support from co-workers is the stimulus that many employees need to take the first step towards a healthier life style. For those employees who are ready to make lifestyle changes, the Booster Break can provide the support needed to begin and sustain a change.

Team Building
In an effort to create a bond among employees, companies often require their departments to attend a variety of workshops. Sometimes they occur during the workday in the workplace and at other times employees are asked to attend retreats in other locations and on weekends. Although these workshops can be effective, changes that occur are often temporary as workers return to their normal work routines, habits, and attitudes. In contrast, the Booster Break happens during the work day as an ongoing activity at the work place. Because workers are sharing the experience, bonds that are formed and reinforced daily can be more enduring. Engaging in

Booster Break activities led by and performed with co-workers as part of the daily work routine, creates relationships that support team building.

APPROPRIATE BOOSTER BREAK SELECTION

To initiate a Booster Break program, we recommend that an organization begin with one Booster Break activity. One activity allows the organization to focus its efforts to successfully introduce and implement the Booster Break program. The choice of activity depends on employee preferences, management support, and available facilities. Once learned or practiced, the activity can be performed at other times during the work day and at home. Based on unique needs, the organization can focus training on one of the following:

Flexibility

Yoga poses and a variety of stretches can be effective in reducing stress and also can relieve cramped muscles caused by sedentary occupations. As Zeer *(2000)* writes in his book Office Yoga – Simple Stretches for Busy People, "The philosophy and practice of yoga comes from India. Yoga basically means union, bringing together the physical, emotional, and spiritual parts of ourselves....Yoga asanas (or poses) help you on many levels: They will strengthen you physically, assisting the digestive, immune, and other bodily systems, and they will empower your mind to be calm, alert, and focused" *(page 9)*. In his book, Zeer *(2000)* provides stretches that can be performed at the work place and designates targeted stretches to address specific problems.

Toning and Strengthening

Isometric exercises can be performed without equipment in work clothes and are effective in toning muscles. "Isometrics require contraction of muscles against resistance, without any change in the length of the muscle fibers.... Isometrics do not make muscles larger, but they do increase muscle strength." *(Davis, Eshelman, & McKay, 2000, page 261)*. Strengthening and toning movements can facilitate everyday tasks as well as prevent soreness and stiffness in your neck, back, and shoulders *(Bradley & Wernick, 2004)*. Strengthening contributes to overall health. A variety of books listed in the appendix offer strengthening exercises you can do at the work place.

Tai Chi

A mind-body practice that originated in China as a martial art. A person doing Tai Chi moves his body slowly and gently, while breathing deeply and meditating *(Tai Chi is sometimes called a moving meditation)*. Many practitioners believe that Tai Chi helps the flow of vital energy called qi *(pronounced chee)* throughout the body. *(National Center for Complementary and Alternative Medicine)*. Potential benefits of Tai Chi are: massaging internal organs, aiding the exchange of gases in the lungs, helping the digestive system work better, increasing calmness and awareness, and improving balance.

(This information was taken from http://nccam.nih. gov/health/taichi/.)

Breath Training

Eastern cultures have extensively explored the power of breath and its effect on the body's energy, known as chi or prana. Breath is a major source of energy supply to the body. Breath training *(also called breath work)* involves achieving change through the use of a special breathing technique known as Connected Breathing. Connected Breathing promotes integration of the physical, mental, and emotional states of being. Conversely, dysfunctional breathing is associated with internal stress, tiredness, and illness.

(This information was taken from

www.wellbeing.com.au/natural_therapies_glossary.)

Relaxation Techniques

Relaxation techniques can reduce negative responses to stress and help you enjoy a better quality of life. These techniques decrease the wear and tear of life's challenges on the mind and body. Practicing relaxation techniques can improve how you physically respond to stress. These changes include: slowing the heart rate, lowering blood pressure, reducing the need for oxygen, increasing blood flow to major muscles, and reducing muscle tension. Additional benefits can be: providing more energy, fewer physical symptoms, and greater ability to handle problems. The main types of relaxation techniques are autogenic relaxation, progressive muscle relaxation, and visualization. The autogenic technique uses visual imagery and body awareness. Progressive muscle relaxation focuses on slowly tensing and then relaxing each muscle group; visualization technique involves forming mental images to take a visual journey to a peaceful, calming place, or situation. Organizations can tailor any of these relaxation techniques to a 15-minute practice for Booster Breaks (www.mayoclinic.com).

Walking the Grounds
Some companies do not have the space or are not able to regularly reserve a conference room. For these organizations walking around the grounds or inside the building as a group is a viable option.

Walking the Stairs
When walking the grounds is not an option, walking the stairs provides another alternative. For this option, weather is not a factor nor is it necessary to reserve space.

The Booster Break Assessment Tool (BBAT)
(Also, see appendix). To streamline the selection process, we have developed the BBAT. Each organization can modify the BBAT to meet its own needs. The purpose of each section of the BBAT is explained below:

Section I. Participant Availability

Section I provides a demographic profile of the workforce. Also, this section addresses the feasibility of one versus multiple Booster Break sessions during the workday to accommodate work shifts. To begin with, we recommend one type of Booster Break.

Section I. Participant Availability

1. What is your position in the organization? (Check one.)

__ Management __ Professional __ Support staff __ Other

2. Do you work: __ Full-time __ Part-time
3. Do you work: __ Days   __ Evenings
4. How many people are in your department/unit? ____

Section II. Experience

Section II addresses previous experiences and helps establish a profile of employees related to potential Booster Break choices. Experiences combined with preferences described in the next section are the criteria to identify the appropriate Booster Break activity. For example, some organizations may choose a new activity as a best choice for a Booster Break, so all employees start at the same level. In contrast, other organizations may select an activity with which most employees have had some experience to capitalize on familiarity.

Section II. Experience

5. During the past 12 months, what has been your experience with any type of physical activity?

__ None __ Some __ Extensive

6. During the past 12 months, what has been your experience with any type of meditation?

__ None __ Some __ Extensive

7. During the past 12 months, what has been your experience with any type of relaxation techniques?

__ None __ Some __ Extensive

8. During the past 12 months, what has been your experience with any type of breath training (breath work)?

__ None __ Some __ Extensive

Section III. Preferences

Section III provides a profile of employee preferences. Assuming that facilities are available, management is supportive, and it is easy to implement, then the top two employee preferences combined with the information on experience can drive the final selection.

Section III. Preferences

9. How interested are you in learning how to do a 15-minute physical activity session with co-workers?

__ Not at all interested __ Somewhat interested __ Very interested

10. How interested are you in learning how to do a 15-minute meditation session with co-workers?

__ Not at all interested __ Somewhat interested __ Very interested

11. How interested are you in learning how to do 15 minutes of relaxation techniques with co-workers?

__ Not at all interested __ Somewhat interested __ Very interested

12. How interested are you in learning how to do a 15-minute session on breath training with co-workers?

__ Not at all interested __ Somewhat interested __ Very interested

Section IV. Leadership

Section IV addresses a profile of employees willing to organize Booster Break sessions as well as Booster Break facilitators to lead the sessions. Leadership qualities include a willingness and commitment to help others, ability to motivate, and an awareness of the importance of health. Employee interest and motivation in organizing and maintaining the Booster Break program are essential.

Section IV. Leadership

13. With proper training, which of the following activities would you be interested in leading? *(Check all that apply.)*

__ Physical activities   __Meditation
__ Relaxation techniques   __Breath training (breath work)
__ I am not interested in leading an activity

14. What experience have you had in leading groups?

__ None __ Some __ Extensive

15. What support would you need from your organization for you to consider becoming a Booster Break facilitator?

_____

_____

_____

16. To what extent are you willing to assist in organizing Booster Break sessions?

        __ Not willing   __ Willing   __ Very willing

Section V. Attitudes

Section V provides data on attitudes related to health-promoting activities during the workday and organizational morale. Attitudes can reinforce or undermine the successful implementation of the Booster Break program.

Section V. Attitudes

17. How important do you feel it is for an organization to provide health-promoting activities during the work day?

        __ Not important   __ Somewhat important   __ Very important

18. To what extent do health-promoting activities during the work day improve organizational morale?

        __ Not at all   __ Somewhat   __ Greatly

Section VI. Availability of Space

Section VI provides important information about the availability of space for Booster Break sessions. This information is critical in assessing the consistency and availability of required space for the Booster Break and effects the choice of activity.

19. Is there available space in your department for five or more people to meet for 15 minutes during each work day?

__ Yes __ No

20. Which of the following areas are near your department and available during the workday for 5 or more people to meet for a fifteen minute Booster Break session?

Conference rooms	__ Available	__ Not available
Cafeteria/dining hall	__ Available	__ Not available
Common areas	__ Available	__ Not available
Hallways	__ Available	__ Not available
Library	__ Available	__ Not available
Stairwells	__ Available	__ Not available
Break rooms	__ Available	__ Not available
Grounds	__ Available	__ Not available
Recreation facility	__ Available	__ Not available
Other_____	__ Available	__ Not available

What Will It Take For My Organization To Get Started?
Quick Reference Chart

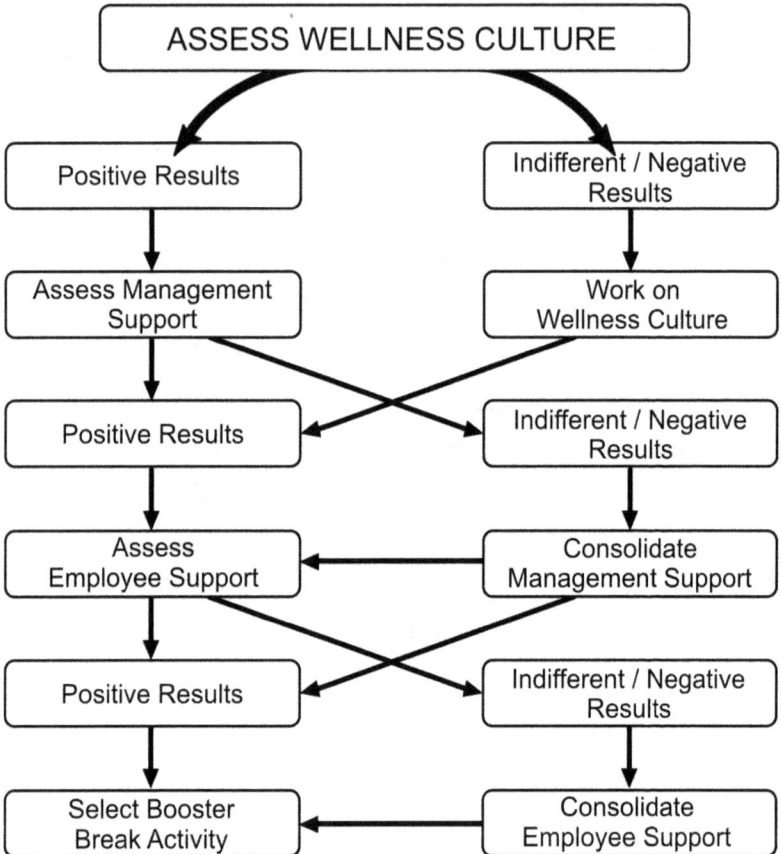

```
┌──────────────────────────────────────────┐
│          ASSESS WELLNESS CULTURE          │
└──────────────────────────────────────────┘
        ↓                              ↓
┌──────────────────┐      ┌──────────────────────┐
│ Positive Results │      │ Indifferent / Negative│
│                  │      │       Results         │
└──────────────────┘      └──────────────────────┘
        ↓                              ↓
┌──────────────────┐      ┌──────────────────────┐
│ Assess Management│      │      Work on          │
│     Support      │      │  Wellness Culture     │
└──────────────────┘      └──────────────────────┘
        ↓                              ↓
┌──────────────────┐      ┌──────────────────────┐
│ Positive Results │      │ Indifferent / Negative│
│                  │      │       Results         │
└──────────────────┘      └──────────────────────┘
        ↓                              ↓
┌──────────────────┐      ┌──────────────────────┐
│     Assess       │      │    Consolidate        │
│ Employee Support │      │ Management Support    │
└──────────────────┘      └──────────────────────┘
        ↓                              ↓
┌──────────────────┐      ┌──────────────────────┐
│ Positive Results │      │ Indifferent / Negative│
│                  │      │       Results         │
└──────────────────┘      └──────────────────────┘
        ↓                              ↓
┌──────────────────┐      ┌──────────────────────┐
│  Select Booster  │      │    Consolidate        │
│  Break Activity  │      │  Employee Support     │
└──────────────────┘      └──────────────────────┘
```

Part II

"The Journey of 1000 miles begins with one step."

Lao Tzu

4
Preparing for the Booster Break

The recommended and preferred method to obtain training for facilitators is to have in-person training by a professional trainer. If a trainer is not available, options two and three below are alternatives.

PHYSICAL ACTIVITY BOOSTER BREAK

There are several ways that participants can learn the techniques involved in the various Booster Breaks. Each approach has pros and cons.

1. Identify a local expert for the selected Booster Break, who can develop a 15-minute series of physical activities at the workplace in work clothes. The expert can either train an employee facilitator who can then lead the daily sessions or the trainer can teach all the participants. The trainer can assure proper form is adhered to and provide personalized guidance for the Booster Break facilitator or the whole group. The

disadvantages are the time and effort required to find the right expert and the costs involved.

2. Purchase a book (such as those listed in the appendix) and have a Booster Break committee select 15 minutes of appropriate activities. This approach is an affordable way for organizations to provide a Booster Break. The committee can review and select one or more books and assess which practices or activities to include. Books may have pictures and descriptions of the steps required and offer a large selection of activities. Specific books can be chosen based on the needs of participants. With a few practice sessions, a Booster Break can be implemented. This option is cost effective and does not require knowledge or selection of a qualified trainer that may or may not be available in the local area. Participants can learn together which can increase cohesion. A disadvantage is that it can be difficult for some people to correctly perform an exercise or activity without seeing it practiced or guided by an expert trainer.

3. Purchase a DVD and select 15 minutes of activities or techniques to use as a Booster Break. Some organizations do not have access to personal trainers or it may be too expensive. The DVD option provides an affordable alternative; however, it would have to be

adapted to the time limit and the circumstance of the organization. As previously described, the advantages and disadvantages for books are essentially the same for DVDs; however, the one advantage for DVDs is that you can see the activity performed and the group can practice until the correct form is achieved.

MEDITATION, RELAXATION TECHNIQUES, AND RHYTHMIC BREATHING

For these activities follow the approach described above. Depending upon the location of the organization, trainers in these techniques may be more difficult to find; therefore, books and DVDs may be the more accessible choice.

Preparing for the Booster Break
Quick Reference Chart

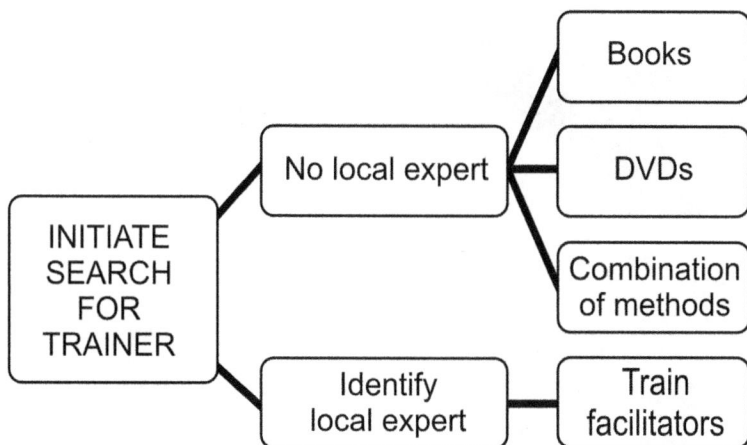

5
Implementing the Booster Break

The first step in implementing a Booster Break program is to form a Booster Break committee. Ideally, this committee is representative of the organization as a whole including employees from all departments and levels of the organization. One of the first tasks for the committee is to identify the most suitable type of Booster Break. Facilitators (employees of the organization) will be trained and in turn will teach the proper techniques and lead co-workers during the Booster Break sessions, or co-workers themselves will be trained by an expert.

Identifying Booster Break Trainers - To assure the success of the program, the selection of a Booster Break trainer to certify facilitators is critical. Even if a trainer will be training the group as a whole, the facilitator will be responsible for assuring that participants have the correct form after the initial training is complete. Depending on the organizational choice, the trainer can teach physical activity movements, meditation, breath work, or relaxation techniques. The trainer should be experienced and certified in the appropriate area and be able to instruct people of various levels. The trainer selection process should involve a committee interview and a demonstration. For many organizations, there are available trainers in the local area. Health clubs, personal trainers, YMCA/YWCA's, community centers, meditation centers, and universities are potential sources. If your geographic locale does not have these organizations, we list resources in the appendix that will enable you to create your own Booster Break.

Selecting Booster Break Facilitators - The selection of Booster Break facilitators is a critical decision for the success of the Booster Break. We recommend that potential facilitators be nominated by management and employees, but self-nominations can be considered. Preferably, the facilitator is someone who is respected in the organization, has leadership ability, is interested in healthy life styles, and is committed to teaching and encouraging others to participate. The final selection of facilitators can be decided by the Booster Break committee. It is inadvisable to coerce or force someone to be a facilitator or participant in the Booster Break because involuntary participation diminishes a sincere and genuine commitment and undermines consistent participation and enjoyment.

Booster Break Pledge - This pledge is designed for the participants. The purpose of the pledge is to secure a public commitment, because research has shown public commitments increase compliance. The key elements of the Booster Break Commitment are to confirm expected benefits from participating in the Booster Break, and to commit to attend four to five sessions per week for a specified time period *(e.g., three months, six months, or a year)*. A sample commitment form is located in the appendix.

Booster Break Buddies - To improve compliance and enjoyment we recommend instituting a buddy system. Each participant should choose a Booster Break buddy to provide support, encouragement, and assist with overcoming challenges. An example of this form is located in the appendix.

Physical Activity Booster Break - Even though Booster Breaks are designed to be safe for all fitness levels, protection from injury is an integral part of the program. Therefore, we recommend all participants complete the American College of Sports Medicine Medical Screening Questionnaire (refer to www.acsm.org) to determine the need for physician approval prior to participating in Booster Break sessions. In addition to the questionnaire, some organizations will have participants sign a liability waiver for legal protection. If liability is a concern, please consult your legal department or an attorney. A sample form can be found in the appendix.

Implementing the Booster Break
Quick Reference Chart

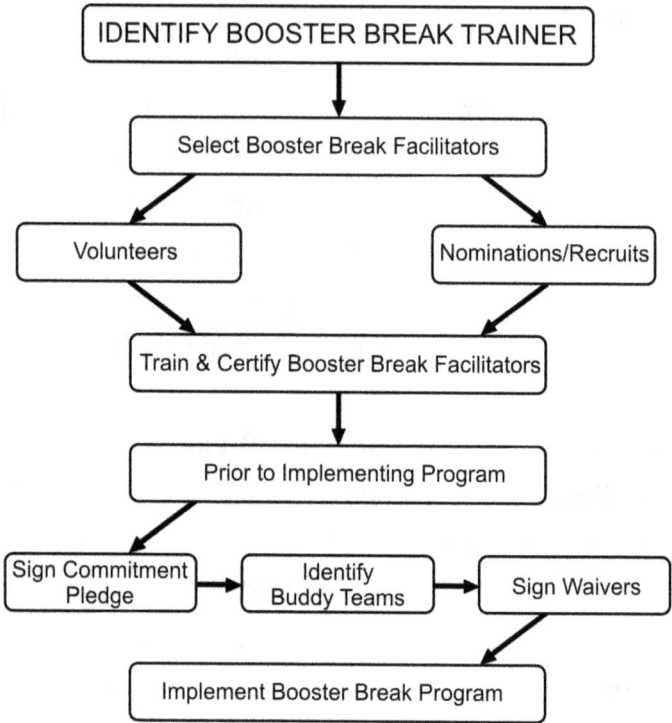

```
┌─────────────────────────────────────────┐
│   IDENTIFY BOOSTER BREAK TRAINER          │
└─────────────────────────────────────────┘
                    │
                    ▼
┌─────────────────────────────────────────┐
│      Select Booster Break Facilitators    │
└─────────────────────────────────────────┘
        ↙                           ↘
┌──────────────┐          ┌──────────────────────┐
│  Volunteers  │          │  Nominations/Recruits │
└──────────────┘          └──────────────────────┘
        ↘                           ↙
┌─────────────────────────────────────────┐
│  Train & Certify Booster Break Facilitators│
└─────────────────────────────────────────┘
                    │
                    ▼
┌─────────────────────────────────────────┐
│      Prior to Implementing Program         │
└─────────────────────────────────────────┘
        │
        ▼
┌──────────────┐   ┌──────────────┐   ┌──────────────┐
│ Sign         │──▶│  Identify    │──▶│ Sign Waivers │
│ Commitment   │   │  Buddy Teams │   │              │
│ Pledge       │   │              │   │              │
└──────────────┘   └──────────────┘   └──────────────┘
                                              │
                                              ▼
                    ┌─────────────────────────────────────┐
                    │  Implement Booster Break Program      │
                    └─────────────────────────────────────┘
```

6
Road to Success
Gaining Momentum

Because the Booster Break can be a minor or major change in the workplace, we recommend consolidating employee and management support. The successful initiation of the Booster Break requires thorough preparation, finalizing logistics, orientation, trial sessions, and an official kick-off.

Preparation - To successfully overcome challenges and barriers to changing workplace culture, the Booster Break initiation and implementation needs a Booster Break facilitator, Booster Break advocate, and/or a committee assigned or appointed to spearhead the Booster Break. This person and/or committee should be fully committed to the program's success.

Logistics - A space (or spaces) scheduled for 15 minutes a day and certified Booster Break facilitators are necessary to begin the program. Because the Booster Break is a low technology innovation requiring no equipment, no additional staff, and no extensive time commitment, the two conditions (i.e., facilitators and space) mentioned above must be in place.

Orientation - We recommend preparing the organization for the Booster Break. One recommendation is to have a small group meeting guided by the Booster Break committee or facilitator to explain the purpose and the expected outcomes. Since time is usually a concern, employees can attend a "brown bag lunch" where they use that time to introduce the Booster Break. Another recommendation is to use the Booster Break Allegory in chapter XI to conduct several book discussions using the discussion guide included at the end of each section. The purposes of the orientation sessions are to inform, solidify support, create anticipation, and respond to questions.

Trial Sessions - We recommend that trial sessions should be conducted for a week or some specified time period to address any challenges before a complete roll-out of the Booster Break program. The trial sessions may include a select group of employees or managers to pilot-test the program and evaluate their experiences after participating in the Booster Break.

Inaugural Event and Celebration - To reinforce and celebrate the importance of the Booster Break for the organization, we recommend a kick-off celebration for the first official day of the program. The type of celebration should be consistent with organizational culture, resources, employee preferences, and management support.

GAINING MOMENTUM

Spreading the Word - After two weeks, one month, or a specified time period, we recommend interviewing participants to assess their experiences, address concerns, and discuss benefits. If appropriate, these interviews can be featured in the organizational newsletter, electronic bulletin board, etc. These testimonials can be helpful in getting others to join and to reinforce participation of those already involved.

Recognition of Participants - Another approach is to recognize current participants/buddies who have achieved the best attendance for one month, three months, and six months. Recognition can provide participants with support for making healthy lifestyle changes. It can include articles in the company newsletter, gift cards, health club memberships, certificates, or other types of recognition.

Communication - Using the newsletter, posting information in common areas, using a company list-serve to circulate updates and accessing electronic bulletin boards can be effective means to generate interest.

**Road to Success/Gaining Momentum
Quick Reference Chart**

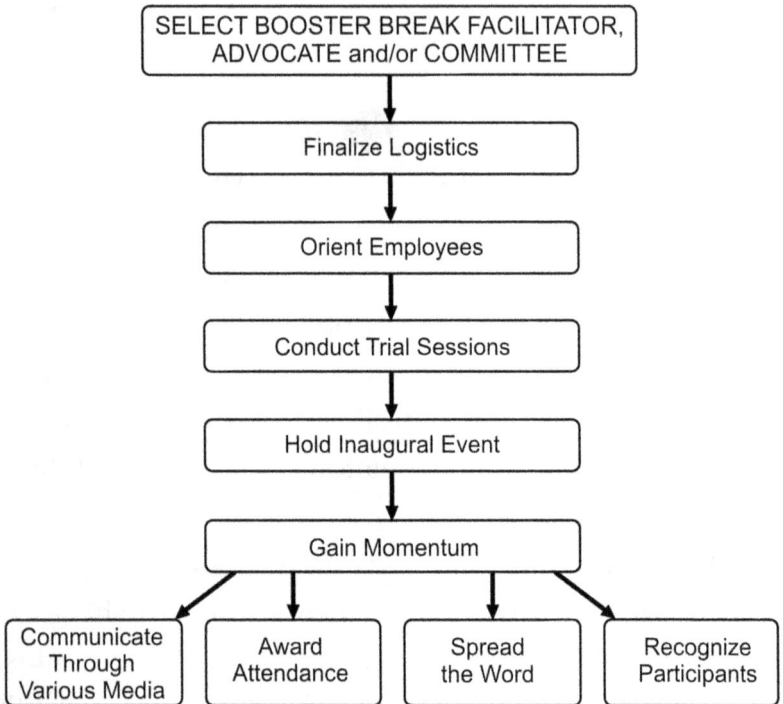

> **SELECT BOOSTER BREAK FACILITATOR, ADVOCATE and/or COMMITTEE**

> Finalize Logistics

> Orient Employees

> Conduct Trial Sessions

> Hold Inaugural Event

> Gain Momentum

| Communicate Through Various Media | Award Attendance | Spread the Word | Recognize Participants |

Part III

"It is not because things are difficult
that we do not dare;
it is because we do not dare
that they are difficult."
Seneca

7
Assessing Booster Break Outcomes

If the organization or Human Resources Department is interested in collecting data to assess the impact of the Booster Break, below are examples of possible outcomes to evaluate.

Physiological Indices - If the company is interested in assessing improvements such as blood pressure, blood lipids, body circumference, height, weight, and other physical measures, we recommend consulting health professionals in your organization, local universities, or medical facilities.

Behavioral Indices - Whatever practice is selected for the Booster Break session, there is a distinct possibility for spillover effects. Employees may continue these practices outside the workday and in so doing improve their overall health. Participants can keep a journal/ diary to record physical activity, meditation, relaxation techniques, and breath training outside the workplace to document their progress, perceptions, and future goals. Additionally, reliable and valid instruments can be administered to assess these practices.

Psychological Indices - If the company is interested in quality of life, depression, stress, anxiety, and energy levels, we have listed websites in the appendix that assess these measures and books that can provide helpful information. Participants can be assessed prior to beginning the program and at various intervals and/or they can be interviewed to determine changes in these indices.

> Because the Booster Break is a group activity it has the potential to enhance co-worker camaraderie, increase team cohesiveness, and enhance satisfaction with the job.

Employee Morale, Job Satisfaction, Healthy Workplace Culture Indices - Most companies are interested in aspects of organizational climate such as employee morale, job satisfaction, and healthy life style support. Because the Booster Break is a group activity it has the potential to enhance co-worker camaraderie, increase team cohesiveness, and enhance satisfaction with the job and organization. To assess employee morale, we recommend downloading instruments from the following website: http://www.confidencecenter.com/morale_assessment.htm

We recommend visiting **www.healthyculture.com** for resources related to promoting healthy workplace culture. An example of an instrument that evaluates the health of the workplace environment is the CHEWS survey *(see appendix – Research Articles)*. This survey can be found in the American Journal of Health Promotion listed in the appendix. We recommend selecting instruments that are reliable *(have results that can be replicated)*, valid *(measure what they intend to measure)*, and easy to administer. In order to assess changes, measurements can be taken at the beginning of the study *(baseline)*, six months, and a year.

Productivity - If a company has clear and/or distinct metrics for productivity, then measures of productivity can be assessed before, during, and after the Booster Break program.

Assessing Booster Break Outcomes
Quick Reference Chart

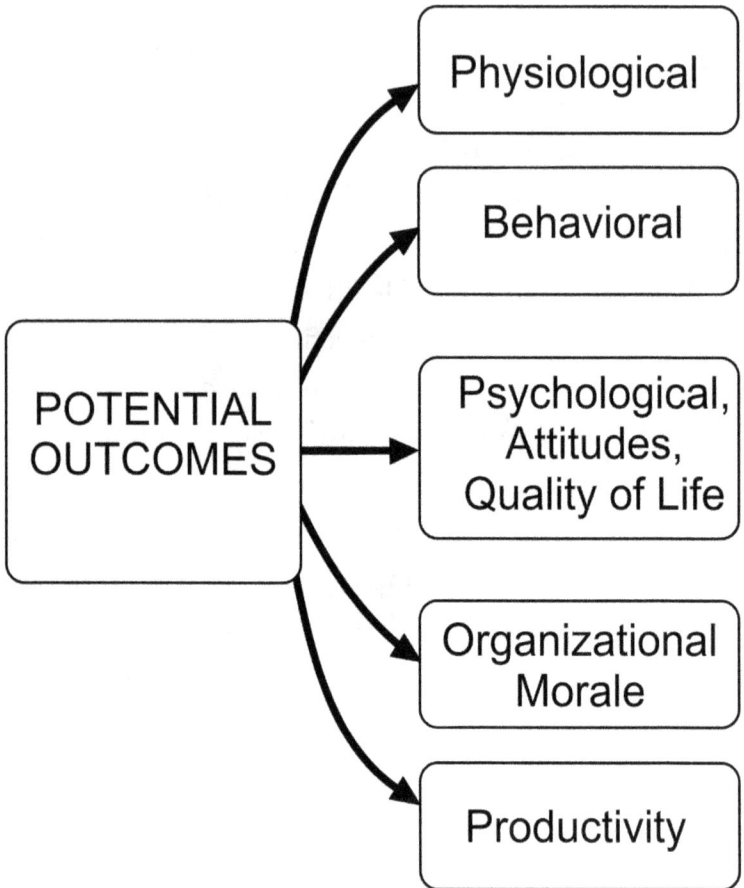

```
                          ┌─────────────────┐
                          │  Physiological  │
                          └─────────────────┘

                          ┌─────────────────┐
                          │   Behavioral    │
                          └─────────────────┘

┌──────────────┐          ┌─────────────────┐
│  POTENTIAL   │          │ Psychological,  │
│  OUTCOMES    │ ───────▶ │   Attitudes,    │
└──────────────┘          │ Quality of Life │
                          └─────────────────┘

                          ┌─────────────────┐
                          │ Organizational  │
                          │     Morale      │
                          └─────────────────┘

                          ┌─────────────────┐
                          │  Productivity   │
                          └─────────────────┘
```

8
Confronting Challenges
Questions and Answers

1. What do you do if employees don't sign up for Booster Break Sessions?

It is important to identify concerns, reservations, and barriers. If the concerns are due to misimpressions or fears related to the Booster Break then these concerns can be addressed through discussions or a trial period. Also, it is important to consider how the Booster Break is promoted. Perhaps the lines of communication have not been effective. Consider other forms of marketing such as posters and flyers in common areas (if permitted by your organization) and encouraging potential participants to attend the Booster Break. Book discussions using the allegory found in chapter XI is another option.

2. What do you do if employees sign up but don't participate in the Booster Break Sessions?

If an employee expresses an initial interest in the Booster Break and does not attend regularly, there may be several reasons. If scheduling is the problem and other employees face the same challenges, the organization can consider additional sessions. If the problem relates to motivation, a Booster Break buddy can provide encouragement. If the problem has to do with work demands the facilitator may be able to offer suggestions.

3. What do you do if it's difficult to schedule a conference room on a daily basis?

If there is difficulty in scheduling, consider alternate spaces such as non-congested hallways, cafeteria, common areas, library, basement, or occasionally accessing large offices. Other alternatives include climbing the stairs or walking the grounds. Also, ask other departments if their spaces are available. *(See Scheduler Form in Appendix)*

4. What do you do if there is not a consensus about which Booster Break to choose?

If there is not a consensus about which Booster Break to choose, one option is to expand the range of choices. Remember any health-promoting practice that can be completed in 15 minutes can be considered. Another option is to periodically alternate the type of Booster Break, for example, every three months or every month.

5. What do you do if no one volunteers to be a Booster Break facilitator?

This problem can be solved by sharing the responsibilities for the Booster Break session on a rotating basis. Another approach is to provide incentives consistent with organizational policies to encourage employees to volunteer for this role.

A Booster Break buddy can provide encouragement.

6. What do you do if the management doesn't support Booster Breaks?

Provide data from this book about the potential benefits of Booster Breaks for the individual employee and the organization as a whole. If you know of other companies that have incorporated Booster Breaks with positive results, inform management about these positive experiences.

7. How does my organization get started? What are our first steps?

The first step is to assess management and employee support. If there is not solid support, book discussions using the allegory provided in this book can help explain the concept. If there is strong support for the Booster Break, then the next step is to identify the preferred type of Booster Break and available resources by administering the Booster Break Assessment Tool (*See appendix*). Once the available resources and preferences are known, facilitators can be identified. Also consult the checklist on page 109.

8. What do you do if more employees want to participate in the Booster Break than space permits?

We recommend two or more sessions of the Booster Break to accommodate morning and afternoon breaks. Consider places other than the conference room (see response to question three). Also, consider offering more than one type of Booster Break, specifically one that doesn't require a room, such as walking up and down the stairs or walking around the building/grounds.

9. How do you hold Booster Breaks when it may conflict with the minimum number of staff required to maintain the office?

We recommend a minimum of five people for a Booster Break session. Each organization has to determine the minimum number of people to maintain the smooth functioning of the office. Morning and afternoon options (or other rotating sessions) can be considered. In small organizations, providing resources for individual Booster Breaks may be necessary (See chapter 9).

10. How do you establish a Booster Break network?

If there are organizations in your local area who

are conducting Booster Breaks, consider establishing a Booster Break support network for managers, employees, and Booster Break facilitators. This network could meet regularly outside of work or communicate electronically to discuss successes, do creative problem solving, and share tips and techniques.

11. What do you do if employees feel coerced to participate in the Booster Break?

We are opposed to any coercion, pressure, or undue influence to participate in the Booster Break because it undermines the core principles of choice and volition. All participants should be volunteers who make a decision based on their personal situations, expectations, and potential benefits.

12. What should you do to change the Booster Break routine if the group would like to alter the activities?

Groups choosing a physical activity Booster Break may decide to change the routine after a period of time. If this occurs, first make sure there is a consensus among the participants for change. If consensus is confirmed, modifications may include different movements, more intense movements, a change in music, or a change in the type of Booster Break.

13. What happens if I'm on vacation, I miss sessions, or I

become pregnant?

We recommend attending the Booster Break sessions whenever you are at work. Because this program is for everyone, there are situations that occur that prevent participation. The important thing is that you resume the Booster Break sessions as soon as you can. If you become pregnant or have other health concerns, consult your health care provider.

14. Why should I participate if I'm already engaging in Booster Break activities on a regular basis?

In addition to individual benefits, there are potential benefits for employee camaraderie and organizational morale. As well, Booster Breaks complement any health-promoting activities practiced outside the work place. Also, the Booster Break can energize participants and reduce stress during the work day.

15. What health conditions would contraindicate participating in the Booster Break?

Booster Breaks have been designed to be safe for all fitness levels; however, if you have any concerns about health conditions, consult your health care provider prior to participating.

9
Solo Booster Break: When Group Booster Breaks Are Not an Option

One of the essential elements of the Booster Break is that it is a group activity. The group provides support, encouragement, and reinforcement for participants; however, some companies cannot have five or more people simultaneously taking their breaks or may have less than five employees. In this situation, we recommend setting aside a space (e.g., table in the break room) to display Booster Break resources. Employees should be encouraged to review the materials and select options best suited to their needs. Employers are encouraged to support co-workers in selecting and practicing Booster Breaks. Although not the preferred method, individuals who are the sole practitioners in their organization can use the materials below.

http://www.centre4activeliving.ca/workplace/trr/tools.html

This website provides information on physical activity at work, including a video with a series of five exercises from four to eight minutes that can be performed in a small space while viewing a computer.

http://ostatic.com/158096-blog/five-apps-to-take-a-break-stay-healthy

This website provides a list of resources to be purchased for those working in sedentary professions. Resources include computer based physical activities that can be performed during work breaks in work clothes.

http://www.acefitness.org/getfit/RubrBndWkout.pdf

This website contains exercises using a Theraband that can be adapted to the work environment. Therabands can be purchased at your local fitness store or on-line and vary according to resistance strength. Therabands are easy to store and use and exercises can be performed in a small space.

Five Good Minutes at Work by Brantley and Millstine, New Harbinger Publications, Oakland, CA, 2007

This book contains 100 stress-relieving and centering activities that can be done within five minutes, at the workplace.

A Moment to Relax by Levey and Levey, Chronicle Books, San Francisco, CA, 2003

This book and CD combination contains breath exercises and relaxation techniques that can be performed at work.

Sometimes, it is not the availability of time or the number of employees to participate that requires a solo Booster Break. Instead, it could be the organizational culture, resistance to change, or unavoidable schedule conflicts.

Karen, one of the authors, encountered this situation at her job site. She tried to get her colleagues to participate in a Booster Break where they would walk around both floors of the building for a total of 10-12 minutes twice a day. Unfortunately, no one was initially interested. By necessity she chose a solo Booster Break and walked the floors of the building herself. At lunch one day she was sharing her experiences with her colleagues, when a new employee joined the conversation and asked if she could walk with Karen. She was a new mother and was having difficulty fitting exercise into her daily routine; the Booster Break was a way to begin to exercise regularly. Both of them noticed that after returning from their walk, they were re-energized and didn't have the expected mid-morning/mid-afternoon slump. Soon another employee asked to join the group. So even if an employee begins the process as a solo Booster Break, that effort can result in a snowball effect, where others may join inspired by the example of one person. Walking the grounds, walking throughout the building, or up and down stairs are good choices.

10
You Could've Had a
Booster Break!

Our hope is that Booster Breaks will become an accepted part of the workplace; because this innovation can provide an opportunity for employees to engage in healthy lifestyle practices at the workplace during the workday, health and well-being are enhanced. The advantages of this approach are that it supports incremental changes and permits individuals to experiment and practice activities on a trial basis that they may not otherwise participate. Also, the Booster Break can capitalize on "teachable or catalytic moments" when an employee wants to make a change, but does not know how to start. Not only can the individual accrue health benefits from engaging in the Booster Break but the organization can benefit as well through enhanced employee morale, job satisfaction, increased productivity, and potentially lower health care costs. If Booster Breaks truly become embedded in the culture, employees taking non-health promoting work breaks *(smoking cigarettes, surfing the internet, consuming coffee, etc.)* may be tapped on the shoulder by a co-worker and told, "You could have had a Booster Break."

We encourage all participating organizations to send us your success stories so we can publish them on our website, **www.BoosterBreaksBook.com**. Send us your testimonials with the subject heading "Booster Break Hall of Fame" and in your email, indicate whether you prefer your testimonial to be published anonymously, with initials, or your name.

Our email address is energize@boosterbreak.com.

Part IV

"In this world we must help one another."
Jean de la Fontaine

"An altruism springs from putting yourself
in the other person's place."
Harry Emerson Fosdick

11
Booster Break Allegory and Discussion Guide

This allegory was created as a basis for a discussion group. Each section is followed by discussion questions. It is up to the Booster Break discussion leader as to whether he or she includes the questions or has an open discussion. Furthermore, the allegory may be read in its entirety or divided into sections and discussed at intervals that fit into the organization's schedule.

Part I - THE PROBLEM

For 10 years, the Evergreen Company had rising profits and the Board of Directors was pleased with the company's performance. The future was promising and the CEO's position was secure, but recently the company had been experiencing some challenges. Employee turnover rates increased dramatically; absenteeism was high; company morale was on the decline; and profits were down. The Board called an emergency meeting to address the situation and the CEO knew he was on the hot seat. The Board demanded a plan to reverse the downward trend.

At the Board meeting, the CEO described his plan to conduct a comprehensive review of each department. Although a necessary step, the Board was impatient and gave him only six months to show measurable improvement. In the immediate future, the CEO had to hire a new Human Resource Manager because the previous manager had accepted a position with a competitor. At first, the CEO was disappointed that the manager had abandoned the company when they needed him most. Upon further reflection, he realized this development was an opportunity. He could hire someone who was innovative, and envisioned the two of them working together to turn the company around.

The CEO began the selection process for the new Human Resource Manager. He received many applications and interviewed the three most promising candidates. He was most impressed with Lindsay. Although she did not have the wealth of experience the other applicants had, the CEO liked her energy, creative thinking, and problem-solving approach, and offered her the position.

Lindsay accepted the position and was looking forward to the risks and challenges of turning a company around. On her first day, Lindsay and the CEO met to develop a comprehensive plan. She suggested administering a needs assessment and an employee satisfaction survey to take the pulse of the company and to learn why morale had declined. The CEO agreed with her suggestions.

Two weeks later they met to review the survey findings. The most obvious conclusion from the survey findings was that poor morale adversely affected every department. The prevailing sentiment was that the company was only concerned with profits and employees were regarded as revenue-producing units. The employees felt that the company didn't care about them. Lindsay knew that this perception was a serious problem and made addressing it her first priority.

DISCUSSION QUESTIONS:
What was your reaction to the results of the survey?

Have any of you ever felt like the employees at Lindsay's company?

Part II - NEXT STEP - SEARCHING FOR SOLUTIONS
The results of the survey indicated that poor employee morale was poisoning the organizational culture, so

Lindsay began a search throughout the industry for innovative ideas to address the problem. The first ideas she found were either too time consuming, too expensive, too trendy, or were short term solutions. To refine her search, she developed specific criteria. The intervention must:

- target only one aspect of the company culture at a time;
- be sustainable over time;
- include all employees;
- occur during the day so it doesn't require staying late, coming in early, or sacrificing a weekend;
- enhance team building, collaboration, and camaraderie;
- fit into the company budget; and
- be evaluated after a trial period.

Having clear priorities was an important first step; but, finding the solution that was based on these priorities would be a challenging and daunting task. Lindsay searched business journals and the internet. She read books on company culture, and attended a conference. She even considered hiring a consultant. After weeks of searching, what sparked her interest most was a conversation with Jack, a colleague, she met at the conference.

Jack was a Human Resource Manager at a large company with an envious organizational culture. Lindsay invited him to lunch to pick his brains. During lunch she explained her company's situation. Some of Jack's suggestions were not appropriate for her medium-sized company, but she was still interested in learning how another company handled a morale problem. Rather than start with the solution, Jack thought it would be more helpful to describe his company's decision-making process.

"We had a problem with absenteeism," he explained "and a big problem with mid-afternoon slump. Work productivity had noticeably declined. We did an exhaustive search to find a solution. We even hired a consultant."

Jack explained, "In order to address the absenteeism problem, the consultant suggested incentive pay for excellent attendance. But, giving a reward months later, was not a strong enough motivator to prevent people from taking days off for personal reasons."

Jack continued, "To counter mid-afternoon slump, the consultant recommended   increasing access to our company work-out facility by adding early morning hours. We implemented this idea, but our facility remained underutilized. We concluded that expecting employees to get to work earlier, even if it saved them the cost of a health club membership was unrealistic.

To address the work productivity problem, the consultant suggested holding a weekend retreat for team building. The problem with a weekend retreat was that it requires giving up a weekend and people have other responsibilities and preferences. Naturally, only a few employees agreed to attend, so we decided not to have it.

Another idea to address work productivity was to give employees the opportunity to make suggestions to improve the company by submitting their ideas to the Human Resource Department. Even though we publicized it by e-mail and the company web site, few people took advantage of it.

The consultant's best suggestion was to administer an employee satisfaction survey; we continue to administer the survey because the results are informative."

Lindsay felt just listening to Jack was saving her company the cost of hiring a consultant. She happily decided to pick up the tab for lunch.

Lindsay then asked, "So what did you do to solve your company's problem?"

Jack explained, "I came across an article that described an innovation called 'the Booster Break.' Because our other options did not pan out, we decided to give it a try."

"What is a Booster Break? I never heard of it," she said.

Jack replied, "The Booster Break is a new way of thinking about break time. As it says in this article, it's '...an organized routine work break intended to improve physical and psychological health, enhance job satisfaction, and sustain or increase work productivity.' Actually, it's a group activity conducted during break time - not before or after work. It can have physical and psychological benefits, as well as improve employee morale."

Lindsay persisted, "I still don't understand. I can't picture it."

Jack replied, "Let's see how I can explain it to you. I began by reading "Booster Breaks: Improving Employee Health One Break at a Time." It's a "how to" book on implementing the Booster Break. I followed their suggestions and first got our managers on board and then our employees. Next I administered the Booster Break Assessment Tool found in the book to determine the best type of break for our company. The choices included meditation, breath training, and physical activity movements. The majority of our employees chose physical activities."

Lindsay inquired, "So your employees get together and do 15 minutes of exercise?"

"No," Jack responded, "it's a little more involved than that. Two employees from our company were selected to be trained and certified as Booster Break facilitators. They learned how to lead 15 minutes of movements that anyone can do."

"OK, but does 15 minutes give people enough time to change their clothes?" she asked.

Jack responded, "That's just it. Booster Breaks can be

completed in 15 minutes in work clothes. The actual break-down is: one-to-two minutes of warm-up movements, ten minutes of strength and flexibility training, and one-to-two minutes of cool down. These movements are carefully selected to avoid injury and are appropriate for most fitness levels. The Booster Break facilitator is trained to encourage participation and promote social support during the session. In other words-it's fun. People want to do it and actually look forward to a Booster Break as a welcome change to their work routine. They get to socialize during their break while doing something positive for themselves. Because they are sharing a non-work experience, it helps with team building and camaraderie as well as morale, and because our management is supporting this, it improves our image."

Lindsay still wasn't convinced but was beginning to see the possibilities.

"You mentioned training. Was it expensive?" she asked.

Jack replied, "Let's just put it this way. Remember that consultant I mentioned? Buying a book for each employee, analyzing the results of the survey, and bringing in a trainer to create a 15-minute series of activities and train our facilitators cost us half as much as the consultant with ten times the benefit."

Lindsay replied," Ok, let's say I'm interested, because as a Human Resource Manager, I can see the potential, but how would I get my employees interested enough to be facilitators?"

Jack responded, "There are several ways. You can ask for volunteers at departmental or company-wide meetings; you can post it on bulletin boards; you can send emails; or you can select two employees who have been identified as having leadership potential. It's important to choose individuals who have the ability to motivate co-workers, communicate effectively, and have good social skills."

Jack continued, "We surveyed our managers and asked them to recommend the best candidates for these positions. I interviewed the finalists and selected two individuals who not only had leadership potential, but a genuine interest in the project."

Lindsay was beginning to consider Booster Breaks as a real possibility but continued to have questions. "How did you get the employees to participate in the sessions?" She asked.

"I had the same concerns." Jack replied. "We had managers meet with their departments to explain the program and how much the company supported it. We anticipated that some people would be reluctant or even resistant to change, so, we knew we needed an incentive. Since we were asking them to give up one of their usual work breaks, we gave participants an extra 15 minutes at lunch time for coming to the Booster Break sessions every day for the first two weeks. We figured that after two weeks they would be hooked."

"Were they?" Lindsay asked.

Jack answered, "Well, a few employees never participated, but our attendance sheet showed that 90% of the employees attended the two-week trial period and almost all of these participants continued after the two weeks ended, even though we no longer gave them the extra fifteen minutes during lunch."

Lindsay interjected, "But you're only talking about two departments. You have a large company. What about the rest?"

Jack responded, "The word spread as our participants became more and more enthusiastic about Booster Breaks. They felt better, had more energy, and because of it, productivity went up- a win-win situation. In fact, there was a spill-over effect. People who never thought they enjoyed physical activity have now, voluntarily, continued exercising after work and on weekends. Even our underutilized work-out facility is getting some action."

"In fact, just the other day I rode in the elevator with Shelly, in Procurement. I complimented her on her weight loss. She told me that the Booster Break was the 'kick in the pants' she needed. Despite the fact that her husband had been nagging her to lose weight for a long time, she had stubbornly dug in her heels and refused. She hated dieting, exercise did not appeal to her, and the constant nagging turned her off."

"At first, Shelly refused to participate when the Booster Break sessions were introduced, but her co-workers' enthusiasm was contagious. She finally decided to give it a try. From her first session, she received encouragement and support. Soon, she looked forward to the Booster Break each day. She even joined her co-workers as they walked during their lunch hour. Previously, a 'junk food junkie,' she now brings fruits and vegetables each day. After three months, her husband noticed a change in her appearance, but he couldn't figure out what it was. Knowing it was a touchy subject, he asked if she had been doing anything different. She told him about the Booster Break. He stopped nagging her and became supportive."

Jack continued, "Last week, I saw Harold, a computer programmer and a confessed workaholic. I was surprised to learn that in high school, Harold was a track star and won state-wide recognition. Now, Harold is married with three kids, works long hours, and has little free time. His health had deteriorated because of his life style and his doctor was concerned. But Harold could never find time to exercise. He thanked me for introducing him to the Booster Break. He loved the idea of doing it at work and not taking any time from his family or his job. Harold told me, 'Doing those fifteen minutes of exercise each day made me realize how much I missed physical activity and how out of shape I was. In fact, I have convinced my family to walk and bike together. Now we're all more physically active and feeling better'."

Jack added, "Departments that didn't have the Booster Break requested the program. They asked if the trained facilitators could share their knowledge with their departments. But part of the reason it worked so well was that the Booster Break facilitators worked in the departments where they led the activities. So we called back the person who had trained the Booster Break facilitators and she trained the team leaders from all the interested departments to become Booster Break facilitators. Since we had prior success, we had several people interested in being trained and certified."

"One thing I haven't heard you discuss is where you hold these sessions," Lindsay inquired.

Jack replied, "You can hold them anywhere there is an available space for 5-15 people arms length apart. We reserve a conference room every day for the Booster Break."

"Isn't that a problem?" she asked.

Jack explained, "In the beginning, the logistics were a challenge; however, we were able to find available conference rooms. It wasn't that difficult. After all, it's only 15 minutes."

"That brings up one last question," Lindsay added, "If the Booster Break is just 15 minutes of physical activity, couldn't a company create its own Booster Break? I mean, how hard is it to figure out 10 to 15 minutes of physical activities?"

"You're right," Jack replied, "we could have tried to do it ourselves, but it would have involved taking the time to research and develop an exercise routine that would fit into those 15 minutes, was safe, and was suitable for a variety of fitness levels. We preferred to go with something that was already proven. It was much more efficient."

Lindsay asked, "Do you think I could observe a Booster Break in action, to get a better idea?"

"Sure," Jack replied. "Our afternoon work breaks are at 2:45."

Two days later Lindsay observed a Booster Break at Jack's company and was impressed by the enthusiasm and camaraderie among the participants. Just observing, Lindsay felt energized. She was sold. Booster Breaks were what her company needed. She thanked Jack and told him her decision. "How should I proceed?" Lindsay asked.

He replied, "The best thing to do is to buy 'Booster Breaks: Improving Employee Health One Break at a Time' and see if it fits for your company, then discuss it with your CEO." Upon her return to the office, Lindsay purchased the Booster Break book and read it that day. Later she shared what she had learned with her CEO. At first, like Lindsay, he was skeptical; however, he trusted her judgment. He thought it was an innovative approach, and could be a step in the right direction to improve poor morale.

DISCUSSION QUESTIONS:

What do you think about Jack's incentive *(offering an extra 15 minutes at lunchtime for two weeks)* to participate in the Booster Break?

What would be your choice of incentives?

Do you think incentives are necessary?

How many of you have been interested in physical activity or meditation but could not find the time?

Can you see the benefits of giving the Booster Break a try?

What do you see as some of the barriers to success at our company? How can these barriers be managed or minimized?

Part III - MAKING IT HAPPEN

The next day, as Jack recommended, Lindsay began discussing the Booster Break concept with several managers. Some were enthusiastic while others were lukewarm about its potential to make a difference. They decided to assess employee interest by providing information on bulletin boards, company newsletters, and departmental meetings. In two weeks, there was enough interest to administer the survey.

When Lindsay analyzed the results of the survey, she found that the poor morale was caused, in part, by high levels of stress, and lack of company support to deal with stress. Employees were not coping well. They felt overworked, and thought that the company didn't care about them. She knew that stress could affect the immune system and considered that it might be partially responsible for high absenteeism, or perhaps people just need a mental health break. Based on the results, Lindsay selected the Meditation Booster Break. By reducing counter-productive stress, she felt employees might be able to better manage their work loads.

After her decision, Lindsay researched methods to train Booster Break facilitators on meditation. She considered holding a study group using a book she found. But instead, she decided to contact a local meditation group and have them create a 15 minute meditation break to her specifications, after which they would train her Booster Break facilitators. Initially, the facilitators would practice among themselves to work out any problems. Then they would train their co-workers. She also purchased copies of the Booster Break book and used the allegory in discussion groups, to help garner more support.

Lindsay and the leaders met with the employees of the two departments to explain the Meditation Booster

Break. During the meeting, the employees asked many questions. For example: "Is participation mandatory?" "Is the Booster Break for both breaks, or just one of them?" "If I don't like it, can I quit? Will I get a better annual evaluation if I participate?" Lindsay and the facilitators patiently answered all the questions. They explained that participating in the sessions was voluntary, designed for one break per day, and was unrelated to job evaluations.

The Booster Break session began and everything was on track. However, the first two week's participation was less than 70%. After the trial period, the Booster Break participants shared their enthusiasm with other co-workers. As a result, participation rate increased to 85%. Lindsay continued to assess the impact of the Meditation Booster Break. She met with department heads to get feedback. On the whole, the results were very positive. Meditation Booster Breaks were helping participants de-stress and because it was the company that enabled them to participate, the sessions improved employee morale. As Lindsay visited the two departments, she could sense a palpable difference in the work environment. The tension had lessened. It was time to re-administer the company's employee satisfaction survey. Although Lindsay was pleased with her observations, to satisfy the CEO, the survey results had to confirm her perceptions.

DISCUSSION QUESTIONS:

Do you think the attendance at the Booster Break sessions for either company was realistic?

What can management do to assure maximum Booster Break attendance including resistant employees?

$$\sim$$

Part IV - RESULTS

Lindsay arranged a time to meet with the CEO to discuss the results of the survey. During the meeting, based on her observations and the survey results, Lindsay described the positive response to the Booster Break sessions, measurable improvement in employee morale, and reduction in employee stress and absenteeism.

"I think the Board of Directors will be pleased with the improvements and these changes took place in less than three months." The CEO smiled.

Lindsay continued, "Just yesterday I had lunch with Carmen, in Accounting, who told me that five months ago, she was 'a basket case.' As a single mother with two kids, there was no relief at home. She couldn't relax. During the Booster Break sessions, she learned how to meditate, which helped her cope with stress. She realized that she hadn't been taking any time for herself and those 15 minutes of meditation helped shift her perspective on life. And even Ralph, in the Sales Department, who laughed at the idea of meditation, admitted that it helped him to relax and concentrate better. He felt more productive. This was the last guy to participate and now he is our poster child."

The CEO responded, "I have a great idea. What would you think about conducting a one-day retreat next month on a work day? In the morning, we could bring in a meditation expert. In the afternoon, we could have a problem solving session to address other concerns related to the work environment and company culture."

Lindsay remarked, "I think that's a great idea. The Booster Break was a beginning step to change our company morale and culture. It has opened communication with employees, so we can work together to make overall improvements." Lindsay then added, "I think it would be more successful if the employees helped us plan the retreat."

After their meeting, Lindsay arranged planning sessions for the retreat. Employees were actively involved in the planning process that resulted in many good ideas and enthusiastic participation. At the retreat, during the morning session, the employees thoroughly enjoyed learning advanced meditation techniques and other ways to relax that benefited them both on and off the job. The afternoon session became a frank and open discussion on how to improve the company. These discussions are still ongoing. The company included many of the ideas the employees had suggested, which in turn made a huge difference in company culture and productivity.

Based on these developments, during the six-month trial period, the Board decided the CEO had made a positive change in the company culture and productivity; therefore, the Board supported his future plans.

DISCUSSION QUESTIONS:

Do you think the developments described in this section can really happen?

Have you ever learned or experienced anything at work that has helped you in your life outside work?

Would you be willing to share your success stories with other employees?

Part V - ONE GOOD TURN

One day, as Lindsay sat at her desk completing a pile of paper work, her phone rang. It was Frank, sounding panicky. Frank had recently accepted a position as a Human Resource Manager with a company in crisis. He was given Lindsay's number by one of the other members of their professional organization.

Frank said, "Lindsay, I hope you don't mind me asking but we belong to the same organization. I was given your number because you had a similar situation to mine. I recently took on this job as a challenge. I thought I could make a difference and now I'm not so sure. Morale is at an all-time low; productivity is down; and the CEO is very concerned. Do you have any suggestions-anything at all?"

Lindsay responded, "The best advice I could give you is to make a list of your priorities and to begin with small changes. Small changes will help you gain the trust of your employees. For my company, the Booster Break worked well as that first step to improve company culture and productivity."

"What's a Booster Break?" Frank asked.

Lindsay replied, "Why don't you treat me to lunch and I'll tell you all about it."

The saga continues....

Addendum

We hope this allegory illustrates how and why the "BoosterBreak" can improve employee health and company morale. In our allegory, the actual implementation of the Booster Break program was intentionally simplified. The intent of this allegory is to illustrate the spirit and potential benefits of the Booster Break program. Companies that are experiencing problems such as those described in our allegory search for solutions. A first step can be to implement the "Booster Break." However, companies that are functioning well also can benefit from implementing the "Booster Break" to maintain and/or enhance their organization's mission and values.

Part V

"If you do what you've always been doing,
you'll get what you've always gotten."
Anonymous

"It's never too late - in fiction
or in life - to revise.."
Nancy Thayer

12
Appendix

About the authors
Wendell C. Taylor, AB, MS, PhD, MPH

Wendell C. Taylor has an AB in psychology, an MS in psychology, a PhD in social psychology, a Masters of Public Health, and has completed a two-year postdoctoral fellowship in Community Health. He has more than 70 publications in scientific journals and over 20 years of university teaching experience. As the originator of the Booster Break, Dr. Taylor is dedicated to creating a Booster Break movement. The objective is for organizations to organize, support, and encourage health-promoting practices during break times.

Karen L. Pepkin, BA, MA

Karen L. Pepkin has a BA in education with a minor in English, and an MA in psychology. For the past 30 years, she has worked in the social service, psychiatric, and education fields. Currently, she is an educational consultant. Her responsibilities include training school district personnel and creating educational products. She is also a published author of two cookbooks, The Best 50 Muffins and The Best 50 Scones *(Bristol Publishing Enterprises)*, and she contributed to developing the scientific publication, "Transforming Work Breaks to Promote Health."

The following forms may be downloaded in letter size format from our website www.BoosterBreaksBook.com

Booster Break Assessment Tool - BBAT

Section I. Participant Availability

1. What is your position in the organization? (Check one.)
__ Management __ Professional __ Support staff __ Other

2. Do you work: __ Full-time __ Part-time

3. Do you work: __ Days __ Evenings

4. How many people are in your department/unit? ____

Section II. Experience

5. During the past 12 months, what has been your experience with any type of physical activity?

__ None __ Some __ Extensive

6. During the past 12 months, what has been your experience with any type of meditation?

__ None __ Some __ Extensive

7. During the past 12 months, what has been your experience with any type of relaxation techniques?

__ None __ Some __ Extensive

8. During the past 12 months, what has been your experience with any type of breath training (breath work)?

___ None ___ Some ___ Extensive

Section III. Preferences

9. How interested are you in learning how to do a 15-minute physical activity session with co-workers?

___ Not at all interested ___ Somewhat interested ___ Very interested

10. How interested are you in learning how to do a 15-minute meditation session with co-workers?

___ Not at all interested ___ Somewhat interested ___ Very interested

11. How interested are you in learning how to do 15 minutes of relaxation techniques with co-workers?

___ Not at all interested ___ Somewhat interested ___ Very interested

12. How interested are you in learning how to do a 15-minute session on breath training with co-workers?

___ Not at all interested ___ Somewhat interested ___ Very interested

Section IV. Leadership

13. With proper training, which of the following activities would you be interested in leading? *(Check all that apply.)*

___ Physical activities ___Meditation
___ Relaxation techniques ___Breath training (breath work)
___ I am not interested in leading an activity

14. What experience have you had in leading groups?

__ None __ Some __ Extensive

15. What support would you need from your organization for you to consider becoming a Booster Break facilitator?

_____

_____

Section V. Attitudes

17. How important do you feel it is for an organization to provide health-promoting activities during the work day?

__ Not important __ Somewhat important __ Very important

18. To what extent do health-promoting activities during the work day improve organizational morale?

__ Not at all __ Somewhat __ Greatly

16. To what extent are you willing to assist in organizing Booster Break sessions?

__ Not willing __ Willing __ Very willing

19. Is there available space in your department for five or more people to meet for 15 minutes during each work day?

__ Yes __ No

20. Which of the following areas are near your department and available during the workday for 5 or more people to meet for a fifteen minute Booster Break session?

Conference rooms	__ Available	__ Not available
Cafeteria/dining hall	__ Available	__ Not available
Common areas	__ Available	__ Not available
Hallways	__ Available	__ Not available
Library	__ Available	__ Not available
Stairwells	__ Available	__ Not available
Break rooms	__ Available	__ Not available
Grounds	__ Available	__ Not available
Recreation facility	__ Available	__ Not available
Other_____	__ Available	__ Not available

Booster Break Participant Commitment Form

Please place a check below to indicate the commitments you are ready to make, and sign at the bottom of this page. Thank you!

___ I commit to being an active participant in the Booster Break.

___ If asked, I will give honest feedback about my experiences with Booster Breaks.

I understand the purpose of the Booster Break and believe my participation will:

___ Energize my day

___ Release tension

___ Afford me the opportunity to try physical activity, meditation, relaxation techniques, or breath training. (circle appropriate activity)

___ Help me make healthy lifestyle choices

___ Reduce stress

___ Enhance my ability to be more productive

___ Other expectations _____

I commit to fully participate in the Booster Break sessions:

___ I will support my Booster Break buddy and the rest of the Booster Break team.

___ I will make every effort to attend a minimum of 4 out of 5 sessions per week.

___ I will continue my participation for at least six months.

_____

Signature of Participant   Date

_____

Signature of Booster Break Buddy   Date

Booster Break Participation Waiver

As consideration for participating in the Booster Break, I, the undersigned, agree that any and all risks to my health including any injury or accident that may occur during the Booster Break sessions are my sole responsibility. I further agree to release and hold harmless *(insert company name)* from any and all liability arising out of my participation in the Booster Break sessions. I will not participate in the Booster Break sessions, unless it is medically safe for me to do so and hereby affirm that my participation in the Booster Break sessions is completely voluntary and not in any way coerced.

_____

Signature of Participant   Date

Booster Break Action Plan Checklist

This checklist is provided to facilitate implementation of the Booster Break. Completing the steps below will assure a successful program.

Preparation

1. Form a committee and/or identify Booster Break advocates (Chapter 5)
2. Assess management and employee interest in the Booster Break (Chapter 3)
3. Solidify support for the Booster Break (Chapter 3)
4. Identify appropriate Booster Break activity (Chapter 3 and Appendix)
5. Select Booster Break trainers (Chapter 5)
6. Select Booster Break facilitators (Chapter 5)
7. Train Booster Break facilitators (Chapter 5)

Orientation

8. Publicize Booster Break (Chapter 6)
9. Schedule/hold discussion groups based on the allegory (Chapters 6 and 11)
10. Develop evaluation criteria (optional) (Chapter 7)
11. Hold Booster Break Celebration/Kick-off (optional) (Chapter 6)

Implementation

12. Begin Booster Break program (Chapter 6)

13. Hold one-month/ three-month/ six-month celebrations for best attendance (optional) (Chapter 6)

14. Publicize Booster Break testimonials (optional) (Chapter 6)

Evaluation

15. Before the program begins, at three-months, and at six months measure Booster Break outcomes (optional) (Chapter 7)

16. Analyze Booster Break outcomes (optional) (Chapter 7)

17. Revise Booster Break program based on participant suggestions (Chapter 7)

Booster Break Schedule Form Example
Week of_____

Booster Break	Facilitator	Room	Hour
Meditation	Mary Jones	2nd floor conference rm	10:15 - 10:30 a.m.
Meditation	Mary Jones	library	10:15 - 10:30 a.m.
Meditation	Mary Jones	cafeteria	10:15 - 10:30 a.m.
Meditation	Mary Jones	2nd floor conference rm	10:15 - 10:30 a.m.

Booster Break Schedule Form
Week of_____

BoosterBreak	Facilitator	Room	Hour

13
Resources and References

This list is not exhaustive. We have selected resources of which we are aware. If they don't meet your needs, feel free to do your own search so that your Booster Break sessions will meet the needs of your organization.

BOOKS

"Stretching" by Bob Anderson
Shelter Publications, Bolinas, CA, 2000

Stretching can be included as a physical activity Booster Break. The following pages are recommended that describe suitable activities- pages 43-48, 71-72, 79-84, 88-91, 92-93, 116-117, 118, 127. These stretches can be adapted to the needs of the group.

"Quick Fit, the Complete 15 Minute No-Sweat Workout"
by Richard R. Bradley III and Sarah Wernick
Atria Books, New York, NY, 2004.

Rick Bradley's activities can be customized for a

Booster Break. Parts 1 and the side bend of part 4 consist of 10½ minutes of the 15 minutes and do not require equipment. This allows for time to get to the session and return to work, if time is essential.

"Five Good Minutes at Work" by Jeffrey Brantley
and Wendy Millstine
New Harbinger Publications, Oakland, CA, 2007

This book contains 100 stress-relieving and centering activities that can be done within five minutes at the workplace.

"8 Minute Meditation, Quiet Your Mind. Change Your Life."
by Victor Davich
The Berkley Publishing Group, a Division of Penguin Group, New York, NY, 2004.

If your organization selects a meditation Booster Break, carefully review this book. Use the extra time to relax and ease back into your work.

"The Relaxation and Stress Reduction Workbook 5th Edition" by
Martha Davis, Elizabeth Robbins Eshelman,
Matthew McKay and Patrick Fanning
Oakland, CA, 2000, New Harbinger Publications.

This book provides simple, concise, step-by-step directions for mastery of meditation, breathing, progressive relaxation, and physical activity.

"Breathe for Life, How to Reduce Stress and Enhance Your Fitness" by Sophie Gabriel

Basic Health Publications Inc., North Bergen, NJ, 2002.

This book is a great resource for Booster Break facilitators if breath training is the organization's preference. On pages 120- 125, Ms. Gabriel describes how to create your own breathing program. Breath training exercises are described on pages 111-119.

"A Moment to Relax" by Joel Levey and Michelle Levey

Chronicle Books, San Francisco, CA, 2003

This book and CD combination contains breath exercises and relaxation techniques that can be performed at work.

"Living Well Therapies" by Henderson J. Smith

Mr. Henderson is a certified Tai Chi and Qi Gong Teacher/ Practitioner who can teach 15-minutes of Qi Gong or Tai Chi movements suitable for Booster Breaks. This website provides general and contact information. www.livingwelltherapies.net.

"Tai Chi for Health and Vitality, An Introduction to Tai Chi" by Barnes and Noble.

This pack of cards provides a variety of tai chi movements that are suitable for Booster Breaks.

"10 Minute Workouts" by Barnes and Noble.

This pack of cards provides a variety of exercises *(with pictures and descriptions)* that target various parts of the body. Some of these exercises can be used for Booster Breaks.

"U.S. Department of Health and Human Services. Physical activity and health: A Report of the Surgeon General." Atlanta, GA: Centers for Disease Control & Prevention. 1996.

"U.S. Department of Health and Human Services. Healthy People 2010: National health promotion and disease prevention objectives." Washington, DC: Government Printing Office. 2000.

The above two reports document studies that show that the majority of Americans do not comply with the Surgeon General's Guidelines for physical activity.

"Sixteen Minutes to a Better 9-o-5 Stress-Free Work with Yoga and Ayurveda" by Vinod Verma
Samuel Weiser, New York, NY, 1999

This book contains a 16-minute yoga practice that can be adapted for a Booster Break.

"Healthy Aging, a Lifelong Guide to Your Physical and Spiritual Well-Being" by Andrew Weil
Random House, New York, NY. 2005

This book presents the benefits of breath work, including a detailed description of a specific breathing technique (pages 29-30, 206, 208-209).

"Natural Health, Natural Medicine" by Andrew Weil
Houghton Mifflin, New York, NY, 1998.

If your organization selects breath training as the Booster Break, this book is a good resource. In chapter 4, page 88 and chapter 6, pages 118-120, Dr. Weil provides instructions for breath work to improve your health. The Booster Break facilitators can decide to include the entire sequence or adapt parts of the sequence for your organization.

"Office Yoga" by Darrin Zeer
Chronicle Books, San Francisco, CA, 2000.

This book provides simple yoga stretches that can be done at work.

⌒⌒

RESEARCH ARTICLES

"Sudarshan Kriya Yogic Breathing in the Treatment of Stress, Anxiety, and Depression: Part II—Clinical Applications and Guidelines."
Brown RP, Gerbarg PL. The Journal of Alternative and

Complementary Medicine 2005;11:711-717.

This article reviews the literature on the positive physical and psychological effects of breath training.

"Alterations in brain and immune function produced by mindfulness meditation."
Davidson RJ, Kabat-Zinn, J, Schumacher J, Rosenkranz M, Muller D, Santorelli SF, Ubanowski F, Harrington A, Bonus K, Sheridan JF. Psychomatic Medicine 2003; 65:564-570

This randomized controlled trial at the worksite showed that meditation improved immune function and positive affect.

"A field study of supplementary rest breaks for data entry operators."
Galinsky TL, Swanson NG, Sauter SL. Hurrell JL, Schleifer LM. Ergonomics 2007;43(5):622-638.

This article studied the impact on productivity of supplemental break times compared to standard break times.

"An effective workplace stress management intervention Chicken Soup for the Soul at Work employee groups."
Horan AP, Work 2002: 18:3-13

This study showed that by developing health promoting programs at the worksite even when not successful, can improve employee morale due to the perception that the company cares about employees beyond their job duties.

"Checklist of Health Promotion at Worksites (CHEW): Development Measurement Characteristics"
Oldenburg, B, Sallis, JF, Harris, D, & Owen, N, American Journal of Health Promotion, 2002, Volume 16 (5), pages 288-299.

This article provides a checklist to assess the extent to which a worksite has a health promoting environment and provides detailed procedures on how to complete the survey.

"Research findings linking workplace factors to CVD outcomes."
Steenland K, Fine L, Belkie K, et al. Occupational Medicine 2000;15:7-68

This article shows the effect of stress at the workplace on cardiovasular disease.

"Transforming work breaks to promote health."
Taylor WC. American Journal of Preventive Medicine 2005;29(3):461-465.

This publication is the original article about the Booster Break.

WEBSITES

These websites were current when the book was written. Please remember that websites often change, so if the topic is of interest, then perform your own internet search.

www.WorkCulture.com
Provides surveys to assess the work culture.

www.BoosterBreak.com
Gives a brief description of the Booster Break concept and references.

www.Wellbeing.com.au/natural_therapies_glossary
Gives a definition of breath training.

hmacheno@coastalnet.com
David Chenoweth, Chenoweth and Associates. Provides information on worksite wellness and health promotion.

www.csep.cal/forms.asp
Provides a questionnaire (PAR-Q) for people 15 to 59 that can be used as a waiver.

www.nccam.nih.gov/health/taichi
Provides information on Tai Chi and other complementary alternative medicine practices.

www.mayoclinic.com
Provides information on relaxation techniques as well as other medical information.

http://ostatic.com/158096-blog/five-apps-to-take-a-break-stay-healthy
Provides a list of resources to be purchased for those working in sedentary professions. Resources include computer based physical activities that can be performed during work breaks in work clothes.

http://www.acefitness.org/getfit/RubrBndWkout.pdf
Contains exercises using a Theraband that can be adapted to the work environment. Therabands can be purchased at your local fitness store and vary according to resistance strength. Therabands are easy to store and use. Exercises can be performed in a small space.

www.applied-meditation.org
Provides information on Heart Rhythm practice, a form of meditation that is appropriate for a Booster Break.

www.preventionminnesota.com/objects/Resources_for_Employers/HLTHYWKPLC/culture12_wrkplc_assess1_23.pdf
Provides an assessment of opportunities for your organization to support healthy behaviors among employees.

www.confidencecenter.com/morale_assessment.htm
Provides a free assessment on employee morale and job satisfaction.

www.centre4activeliving.ca/workplace/trr/tools.html
Provides information on physical activity at work, including a video with a series of five exercises from four to eight minutes, that can be performed in a small space while viewing a computer.

Additional copies of this book may be
purchased through our website:

www.BoosterBreaksBook.com

Need a copy for everyone in your organization?
Contact us at energize@boosterbreak.com
to ask about quantity pricing for 50
or more copies of the book.

Visit our website for more information about Booster
Breaks, and resources you can use to implement
your Booster Break program, including downloadable
forms, printable certificates, and more.

Wendell C. Taylor, PhD, MPH and Karen L. Pepkin, MA
are available for consulting and speaking engagements
with your organization. For more information,
contact them at energize@boosterbreak.com.